I0839736

America
Yesterday…Today…Tomorrow

Discovering the Truth About Socialism

Jane Scoggins Bauld

Under the Green Umbrella Publishing
Copyright 2019 Jane Scoggins Bauld
ISBN: 9781798758892
Alll Rights Reserved
Printed in the USA
1.Children 2. American History
3. Socialism 4. Capitalism

DEDICATION

Dedicated to Annie and Braden,
my faithful prayer warriors for America,
and any "tomorrow" who will pray for
America.

PREFACE

America's children are our future—our tomorow.

Today, they are being "educated" —indoctrinated—
in public schools and are taught that America is unjust.

They are being taught that capitalism is an unfair economic
system, outdated for an elite society. and must be
replaced quickly by Socialism.

This viewpoint is taught in public schools, universities,
 in the news media, and online.

We believe that America's past is noble and that America is noble.

This essay represents the attempt of a well-known children's
author to teach children—through their parents—a different
message, a true message of America's greatness.
A message of what America has been,
what America is,
and what America will be.

It is the author's hope that parents will realize the doomed
system of Socialism leads to destruction, and that you will join efforts
to speak out against this false teaching in our schools.

Most importantly, it is the hope that Americans will humble
themselves and pray. Only then will God heal our country.

*"All tyranny needs to gain a foothold is for people of good
conscience to remain silent."*
—Thomas Jefferson

Jane Scoggins Bauld is an award-winning pre-school and kindergarten teacher and the author of more than twenty books for children. She is especially well known for her *Hector's Escapades* series featuring the Austin bat colony, for her books about the Taniguchi Oriental Garden (*The Story of Mother Tree* and the *Journey of the Third Seed*), *The Seasons of Treaty Oak* (about the historic Treaty Oak in Austin), and *Rights for Children*, for which she was invited to give a book-signing at the United Nations in New York. She also has written a series of Christian books for children. Her first venture into the genre of political essay is:

AMERICA

YESTERDAY...TODAY...TOMORROW

Yesterday

My 11-year-old grandson Braden and I sat down one day and talked. We talked about America. I could see that in the government public school he goes to, he had learned nothing about the foundation of America. It seemed important that he know, so he could appreciate our country.

I asked Braden what type of government we had.
He said, "A democracy."

"No" I told him. "We have a Democratic Republic. Our forefathers came to America to be free, to set up a government to ensure freedom."

In their home country of England, many of their freedoms were being taken away, including the freedom to worship God as they pleased. The big government was turning against individual freedom and demanding more control and more taxes.

With great courage, they dared to travel across the Atlantic Ocean to a New World they had heard about.
"There we will be free!" they declared.

They made the journey with their families and set up small settlements. Soon they were ready to establish a government that would assure they would never be required to give up their freedom.

They wrote a Constitution setting out limits and requirements for the new Democratic Republic over 200 years ago. Founding Father Benjamin Franklin said,

" We have a Republic if you can keep it."

In this Republic, each state in America would get to vote for the person or persons to go to Washington D.C. to represent them, either as a Congressman or as a Senator.

Congressmen and Senators work for the people from their state who vote them into office, and their job is to do what the people from their state tell them to do.

Our forefathers established a **capitalist system** of economics, designed to keep government small and responsive to the people. Our new government was to be by the people, of the people, and for the people. Opening words of the Constitution: ***"We the people of the United States"***

A capitalist system gives individual freedom for each person to own property, own a business, and to do business as they please, not dictated by government.

Sometimes, when representatives we voted for get to Washington, they begin to feel too important. They do their own thing, instead of doing the will of the people who sent them there.

That is why we the people must keep watch. We must be diligent to see that our government stays small and responsive and limited. We can vote those out of office who break those rules.

The Founders set up three co-equal branches of government:
        Executive   (President and Vice President)
        Legislative   (Senators and Representatives)
        Judicial   (Courts)

These three branches were designed to work together to keep America strong, and to keep our government from getting too big and too powerful!

The Founders realized it would be hard to maintain. Outside forces would come in and try to take over— to change our government. Sometime forces from within our own government would try to take over, proudly pronouncing,
"We want to fundamentally transform America."

What if we don't want our government changed? What if we like it the way it is? The Founders wisely put in safeguards to prevent takeovers from happening.
They wrote
the Constitution.
the Declaration of Independence.
the Bill of Rights.

These three documents were signed and brought forward to create a new country—the United States of America—a country founded on Christian principles.

No country in the world had **ever** been founded on Christian principles. No country had ever been founded that insured freedom for all. America is unique.

God has His hand over America.
He has blessed her and protected her.
He is still protecting her to this day.

But it takes a watchful eye from the people of America to ensure that she will be safe from takeover!

"All tyranny needs to gain a foothold is
for people of good conscience to remain silent."
—Thomas Jefferson

A Capitalist economy, under our Democratic Republic, believes in small government, with the people in charge. The people are the boss! They vote for their congressmen and the President to do their will.

Just to be sure we understand it, let's see what Webster's Unabridged Dictionary says about capitalism.

"Capitalism is an **economic system** characterized by **private ownership** of capital goods by investments that are determined by **private decisions** rather than by state control, and by prices, production and distribution of goods that are determined by a **free market**."

A Capitalist government believes in a Free Market. No government control. That means any person can start a business and run it as they please. They can make money and spend it as they please. They can find a job anywhere they like, and change jobs if they like.

A Capitalist government allows everyone to own a home or property of their choosing. They are allowed to have private property and do with it as they like.

Our Democratic Republic insures in the Bill of Rights
      freedom of speech,
          freedom of movement,
             freedom of religion,
                freedom to own guns,
                   freedom of ownership,
                     freedom of the press,
                       and freedom of voting.
Ours is a government **Of** the people,
             By the people,
                and **For** the people.

There are other forms of government in the world, but they do not allow the freedoms our Democratic Republic offers.

We hear much in today's news about Socialism. Socialism is the opposite of our Democratic Republic.

Socialism has been tried throughout history in several countries, such as Russia and Cuba. It has failed every time!

Let's see what Webster's Unabridged Dictionary says about Socialism:

"Socialism is a **political movement**, advocating **government ownership** and administration of the means of producing, and **control** of the distribution of goods. It is a society of group living in which there is **no private property.** The means of production are **owned and controlled by the government.**
Socialism is a **Marxist theory of _transition_ between capitalism and communism.**"

Socialism believes in big government with total control. Socialism does not allow anyone to own private property. All property, including homes, belong to the government.

Socialism does not allow anyone to own a business. All businesses are owned and run by the government. Government decides where one works, how much money they make, and how much taxes to pay to the government.

Socialism does not allow for freedom of speech or freedom of the press. The government oversees television and radio, and tells them what they can and cannot say.

Socialism does not allow for freedom of movement.

Socialism does not allow for freedom of religion.

Socialists say the Constitution of the United States is outdated, that it is not relevant for a modern society.
They want to do away with it.

The founders of America would disagree. They designed the Constitution to stay true forever, as long as there is an America.

For many, many years, socialists in our government have tried to change our governing system.

Sometime they call themselves Democrats.
Sometime they call themselves Progressives.
Today, they call themselves Socialists.

The names may vary, but the purpose does not. They want to transform America from a Democratic Republic into a Socialist State. They work patiently, persistently, to transform America from its founding principles—
a government **Of** the people.
By the people.
For the people.

If this change is allowed, it will be the downfall of the greatest country in the world, **America,** and possibly the downfall of the whole world.

Where are the American people while this is going on? Don't they notice that our America is threatened?

People are busy. In their freedom, they are working, making money, and buying stuff. They seldom give a thought that America is undergoing change. They believe America will stay the same forever.
"Don't worry. Be happy."

One of the early changes Socialists made was to declare the child property of the government, not the parent. They gave the government the right to decide what was best for the child, where they would go to school, and what they would learn.

They organized an Education Department. Now government decrees what children learn. They removed all signs of Christianity. There is no mention of prayer or Christmas or Patriotism in a government school.

Instead of parents and local leaders deciding what children should learn, government "experts" set the curriculum, naturally to support the goal they are reaching for—Socialism.

In the first grade, Braden was not allowed to tell about his invitation and attendance to Republican Governor Greg Abbot's Inauguration.

And where are concerned parents? They are apathetic!

We are like the song <u>Row, Row, Row Your Boat</u>
"Merrily, Merrily, Merrily, Merrily, Life is but a dream."

We never believed America could become a Socialist State.

Years ago Universities began to hire Socialist professors who could easily brain-wash young people away from home for the first time.

Socialists set the curriculum for High Schools, Middle Schools, Elementary Schools, and even Pre-Schools.

They organized Post-Natal supervisors to visit homes of newborn babies. If the supervisor did not approve of something the parent was doing, they had the power to take the child away from the parent.

Socialists control the media. They send "talking points" for news media to broadcast. These talking points are often untrue! Their propaganda is repeated daily!

Socialists began to take over health care. I was in High School in the '50's, and even then they sent us pamphlets describing how wonderful Socialized Medicine was—controlled of course by the government!

They forgot our country was founded on the premise of **small government** and **individual freedom**! Rapidly our government is morphing into **big government.**

We need to reflect on the fact that every institution government takes over becomes inefficient, expensive, and corrupt—the schools, the media, the post office, the tax department, and health care, and even the Federal Bureau of Investigation.

"A well-instructed people alone can be
permanently a free people."
       —James Madison

Then there is college tuition. In the "old" days, students worked and saved money to pay college tuition. With help from parents, they felt independent.
Independence is an enemy of Socialism!

So the Socialists came up with a plan. Students today easily take out a loan from the **government.** Tuition has skyrocketed and loan debt has skyrocketed! Now students are deeply in debt to the government.

A dangerous place to be!
Another erosion of our Democratic Republic.

Our America is slowly, but methodically, being eaten away by Socialism. We need to decide if that is really what we want before it is too late. It can be stopped!

Since the dictionary's description says that Socialism is a **transition period between Capitalism and Communism**, let's see what the definition of **Communism** is.

"**Communism is a theory** of social and economic **organization advanced chiefly by Karl Marx**. It advocates **public ownership** of means and production, as factories and resources, the sharing of the products of labor, the establishment of a society in which competitive and social classes disappear. It is the establishment of a classless society in which resources are commonly owned (by government) and used for the benefit of all."

We might notice that **Capitalism is a system**. Both **Socialism and Communism are political theories!** A theory is an idea that might or might not be true. It is an idea that can change for the convenience of those in power.

Today

Today, Socialists smell victory. They are almost finished with the **fundamental transformation of America.** They are on the brink of turning our Democratic Republic into a Socialist State, controlled, not by and for the people, but by and for big government.

 Big government will make every decision for us.

Since Socialism is described in the dictionary as a political theory, it is necessary to look at some political tactics in today's government.

This transformation theory comes directly from a Chicago professor, Saul Alensky. He wrote <u>Rules For Radicals</u>.

Alensky dedicated the book to Lucifer, who is Satan! Satan was named Lucifer before our God hurled him out of heaven for his evil ways!

Not many years ago in our Texas Capitol, two groups were there:

The conservatives were singing, "Amazing Grace." The liberals were chanting, "Hail, Satan!"

Do Socialists really worship Satan? They won't admit it, but their plan comes from this book.

As we found earlier, Socialism has been tried in several countries and has **never** worked! It always ends in disaster. Could it be a **false theory**?

Several decades ago socialists in our government began to take away land that belonged to private citizens or to a state. Their land now belongs to the government. This land-grab continues.

Here are some things that are happening **today** to further the Socialist movement:

Socialism: all property belongs to the government. Government continues to take private land in the western United States and declare it government property.

Socialism: all businesses owned by government. Government is taking control of many private businesses and shutting down others.

Socialism: believes in wind and solar power for energy to run cars and warm homes. Coal and oil and gas production will be eliminated.

If Socialist government directs the tax service, (the IRS), they can charge any amount for taxes.

Socialists in the FBI directed the wire-tap of conservative groups, to listen to phone messages and on-line messages

"I am committed against any attempt to rule the free people."
—*Daniel Webster*

Just this week: February 2019

Socialists in the Congress of our government
announced a new declaration called
The **Green New Deal**. Here it is:

Within 10 years oil, gas and coal will be totally shut down. There

will be solar and wind energy only.

Electric cars only! No gas motored cars allowed.

No airplanes.

No cows! (Yes, they believe cows cause pollution.)

No one should have a child. It is bad for the climate.

Every building and home in America must be remade
to conform to climate change regulations.

Why do we even listen to these absurd ideas?

Because they are a novelty
and everyone is intrigued with novelty!

The ideas are presented in animated and positive ways,
designed to persuade people that, even though they bring
drastic changes, they will make everything wonderful!

It will bring utopia to the whole world!

But the novelty is not believable. It is not good.
These fake "theories" of Socialism are extremely dangerous
and even life-threatening.

A recent poll shows that a majority of college students have a favorable view of Socialism.

Could it possibly be due to things they have learned in government schools for the past sixteen years?

Is this the America our Founding Fathers established?

No it is not! It is not our Democratic Republic!

As election time approached for a new president in 2016, the then-current Democrat President, Barak Obama, supported Hillary Clinton to be the next president.

She is a "Democratic" Socialist, a student of Saul Alensky. Her victory would quickly bring transformation from our Democratic Republic to Socialism. Very soon we would be the Socialist State of America.

But that's not the way our Republic was established. Our president is not a King. Our president cannot appoint anyone to replace him as President!

Every four years the people of America vote for the next president. The current president can be re-elected for another term, but two terms, and only two terms, is the limit!

The Socialists still believed Hilllary Clinton would win easily, and the transformation of America was on the verge of being accomplished.

No more free America!

Tomorrow

Something happened on the way to the voting booth. **The Hand of God**. God raised His mighty right hand to protect America.

God loves America because it is a Christian nation.

He stopped the Socialists by using an unsuspecting American businessman, Donald J. Trump. Donald Trump loves America, and he was sad to see it being turned into a Socialist State. He was willing to help save her.

Donald J. Trump was elected.

Hillary Clinton was defeated.

But the Socialists weren't through. They planned a revolution called the **Resist Movement.** They would resist anything President Trump did to restore America to its founding principles.

But, with the Hand of God, Donald Trump never gave up. The forgotten people of America, the silent majority, stood up. They humbled themselves, and prayed. They faithfully prayed that America would remain strong.

11 Chronicles 7:14

"If my people who are called by my name will humble themselves and pray, and seek my face, and turn from their wicked ways, then will I hear from heaven, will forgive their sin, and will heal their land."

This is a time for prayer.

Do you remember what Jesus asked His disciples to do as He prayed in the Garden of Gethsemane the night before His arrest? He asked His disciples to pray.

He said, "Stay alert and pray."
But when he returned to them, they were asleep!

God is telling us, "Stay awake and pray." Pray for America to remain free for many tomorrows.

When Braden was starting into Fifth Grade, I asked him what I could pray for in his new school year.
He wanted me to pray that he wouldn't get in trouble!
"Sometimes I talk at the wrong time, and the teacher doesn't like it."

We prayed. After the first day of school I asked him how it went. He told me a story of a visual image that was an answer to our prayer.

A new boy had come into his class, and this new boy talked too much. He was loud and disruptive. Braden watched. He said the teacher got really angry with the boy.

We prayed for him.

A few days later Braden took him aside and had a quiet talk with him. He told him when to talk, and when the teacher needed him to be quiet.

The boy listened, and thanked Braden for helping him.

God had given Braden a visual image of his very own problem. He didn't like what he saw. He has not gotten into trouble a single time the whole year!

God has given Americans a visual image of Socialism
It is the country of Venezuela.

Venezuela was once a rich country with lots of underground oil reserves, which they sold all over the world.

The people had plenty, they worked, they were happy, they were free. Tourists visited the country, which is on the ocean-front of the Gulf of Mexico.

But something happened to Venezuela. A Socialist dictator usurped the President of Venezuela and forced him to leave the country.

Then the Socialist dictator took over radio and television. Now the only news is what he allows.
No more freedom of the press.

He took ownership of businesses.
Now he can hire only those who support him.
No more free enterprise.

He took over all personal property.
No one owns a home, a car, or any material goods.
He took over the military, to enforce his Socialism

Venezuela quickly went from riches to rags. People are homeless, starving, and dying. Americans sent trucks of food, but the Socialist dictator had his military burn the trucks with all the food inside.

Starving families stood by and watched helplessly.

But a few weeks ago, the people rebelled. They took to the streets. They want their country back and they are willing to stand up and fight for it.

They are willing to pray for it.

This visual image of what can happen in America is haunting. Socialism does not work. Socialism has never worked. Not in Russia. Not in Cuba. Not in Venezuela!

Everyone is poor.
      There is no freedom.
            There is no hope—no future.

Braden and all our young people are our **"tomorrows."**

If you are reading this, you are our **"tomorrow."**
     You are our prayer warrior, praying for our country.
     You must decide whether you want a
          Democratic Republic or Socialism.

Our **"tomorrows,"** please remember how treasured America is. Please remember how important it is to keep alert.

I believe our **"tomorrows"** are brave enough to do the job. If they do, they will still have the Constitution and the Bill of Rights. We will still have our freedom.

We will pray for our **"tomorrows."** Our heroes.
     And we will pray for America.

*"Only a virtuous people are capable of freedom.
As nations become corrupt and vicious,
they have more need of masters."*
             —Benjamin Franklin

All Americans, and all our **"tomorrows,"**
we are a good people.
America is a good country.
We are still free!

We can proudly stand,
with our hand on our heart
and pledge allegiance to our beautiful
red, white, and blue American flag.

I pledge allegiance to the Flag

Of the United States of America,

And to the Republic for which it stands,

One nation under God,

Indivisible,

With Liberty and Justice for all.

May God Bless You,

May God bless our **Tomorrows**

And may God Bless America.